THE BREADCRUMB TRAIL

THE BREADCRUMB TRAIL
A POETRY COLLECTION

Jane's Studio Press
Design by Jane Cornwell
www.janecornwell.co.uk

ISBN: 978-1-7384960-0-6
Also available in hardcover and Ebook format.

More poetry from
Jane's Studio Press

Keeping Afloat
by Samantha Terrell

Wonderland in Alice
Plus Other Ways of Seeing
by Paul Brookes

Tiger Lily
by Susan Richardson

Othernesses
by Paul Brookes

Confronting The Elements
by Samantha Terrell

FOREWORD
BY SUSAN RICHARDSON

"... I am left

to lever words like windows

until they open

onto the land I walk in dreams"

-from By Phonelight

When I first read Lawrence Moore's poetry, I felt transported into a different time, into unexplored realms and new landscapes of imagination. The Breadcrumb Trail delivers these sensations with the magical, musical flourish, and unwavering love that only Lawrence can conjure. It is like no other experience you will ever have and no other place you will ever go.

If I had the pages, I would quote every poem in this collection. I would record every reaction, every smile, every tear, every moment of held breath followed by exclamations of wonder. How does one begin to write a foreword for a collection like *The Breadcrumb Trail*? Do I approach it with an academic bent? In a linear fashion? Or, do I write about how Lawrence's poetry makes me feel, share lines that take my breath away, that transport me into the very special world only Lawrence can create?

"We wake with strange dreams on our tongue"

-from Our Discordant Song

The Breadcrumb Trail begins with what feels like an invitation, a lovely teasing taste of what's to come. It is a beginning with open eyes and a curious heart. It beckons you, makes you want to know more, to discover more. This is an invitation you will eagerly accept.

"Long after darkness first strolled out to play,

we cut the torches, possibly to sleep,

convinced all other lights were slunk away,

not counting on the hours forests keep."

-from You Needn't Search Alone

In this collection, Lawrence Moore is your guide on a quest, an uncovering of truths long hidden, an unfurling, a blooming. *The Breadcrumb Trail* is, in so many ways, an homage to nature and all of the magic to be discovered there. In poems like, *You Needn't Search Alone,* nature is not just a backdrop, not just a canvas, but a character, alive with sound and pulse, playfulness and wickedness, joy, generosity and wisdom. This truth is painted boldly and with suspense from the first tastes of an unforgettable adventure.

"I was born from an acorn, scattered far

by a seldom recounted shooting star.

Very near to this forest, I spied my way.

There are other ones like me, the ravens say.

I was never a boy, not exactly girl,

I will rarely be found in a concrete world."

-from Miniature Garden

All of the poems in *The Breadcrumb Trail,* are rooted in the special musicality that only Lawrence Moore can bring. He is a master of the melding of words and sound; his poetry is storytelling at its most rhythmic and beautiful. Lawrence wields language as if concocting a potion. His is a cauldron filled with generous heaps of wonder and imagination, a lovely hint of danger, and always love. In quintessential Lawrence Moore style, poems like, *"Miniature Garden"*, highlight his deliciously wonderful brand of poetic storytelling.

"There are rumours of death in the word goodbye".

-from The Word Goodbye

Although there is an undeniable sense of whimsy in Lawrence's writing, there are also notes of darkness and caution, felt in poems like *The Word Goodbye.* This thread continues in, *The Axeman,*

"Gather your loved ones

and press them well

to stem the trickling of their cares"

and, *Screw the Thorns.*

"Pick up those trembling, weary legs and run

while calories and limbs remain your own.

You've had one glimpse, you need to stop at one

else sanity decides to flee alone."

The breadcrumbs that lead you through this collection and bind it together as a whole are both complex and enchanting, joyous and frightening. There is a sense of freedom, but also within that freedom, at times a contented loneliness.

"I feel so very lonely

and alive"

-from Interstellar

All along *The Breadcrumb Trail,* bringing Lawrence Moore's poems into even more striking focus, are the beautiful drawings and paintings of Jane Cornwell. I knew from the moment I saw Jane's artwork, that she and Lawrence would make a stellar creative team, and this collection of poems and illustrations delivers in over-flowing pots of artistic gold.

"I come to this place

for contradictions,

mutations,

curveballs,

to offer memories

of my lost

for the aid of my must be found"

-from By Phonelight

The Breadcrumb Trail is a masterfully woven journey of juxtaposition. Throughout, there are complimentary threads of heroism and wickedness, hope and fear. There is delight in the unknown and in the act of discovery. Where there is life, there is also a threat of demise, and underneath the darkness, there is always light. Through his poetry, with nature as his guide, Lawrence Moore, magically, makes sense of this.

"Beneath the darkness there hides a gentle soul"

-from Beneath the Darkness

Under the whimsy, the delightful mischief and the flashes of danger, there is, in Lawrence's poems, always a sense of reverence, roots of vulnerability, trust and love. In poems like *Dark Ancient Woods,* and *One Tiny Anonymous Speck,* these feelings are so strong for me, I find myself crying every time I read them. The language is beautiful, the stories captivating. Simply put, Lawrence Moore's poetry takes my breath away.

"I'm just hoping

one day

we can fade and fall apart together,

one tiny anonymous speck

blending into the background of our choice"

-from One Tiny Anonymous Speck

In the poem, *Boy Number One,* Lawrence writes, ***"We don't all want to know how magic is done."*** I love the freedom in this line, the sense that it's ok to just be in the magical moments, and what Lawrence has created with *The Breadcrumb Trail* is most definitely magic. As long as I can return to this world, again and again, I am happy simply knowing that his poems make the world a better and more beautiful place.

FOR MATTHEW

CONTENTS

OUR DISCORDANT SONG

We wake with strange dreams on our tongue.

Still far from dawn, we strain our eyes.

A thousand sets return our gaze,

us wayward pups to analyse

and what they see, we see ourselves

unfiltered by the go-to tricks.

No pageantry to spare us now,

no mobile phones, three slipper clicks.

The owls, it seems, are lost in thought,

the ravens cackle from their nests,

the field mice huddle, deep in holes,

the roebucks flee and we are left

to ponder our discordant song

of tyranny and tenderness.

YOU NEEDN'T SEARCH ALONE

Long after darkness first strolled out to play,

we cut the torches, possibly to sleep,

convinced all other lights were slunk away,

not counting on the hours forests keep.

Upon this tent, most subtleties and hints

have made these skittish fools recoil and hide,

but when it came to dreamy purple glints,

we couldn't fight the urge to steal outside.

We saw them as they rushed between the trees
to watch us back while softly treading air.
Small children graced with wings they might have been
without the signs of struggle in their stares.

They cradled words long shaped for us to hear,
then slowly let them out in dulcet tones,
with nothing landing plain to human ears
except the phrase 'You needn't search alone.'

We slithered onwards, strove to comprehend,
incredulous and dumb, but keen to learn.
Their lights went out, still yet to glint again
upon this tent, though often we return.

RAINDROP AND RUBY

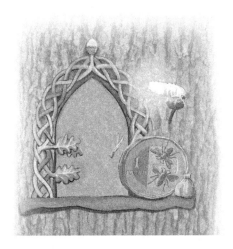

What must the tooth fairies think?

Not the prefects

who obligingly take shape

beside the sleeping child's pillow

to perform a graceful swap

and fleet escape,

but those who entered fairy school

with talents too unruly,

now left to lug

their plate-sized coins

like Raindrop in search of Ruby?

What will she surmise
on dodging sozzled revellers
and strange metallic tubes
unheard of in Victorian times
when last they turned her loose?

When she levers
onerous letter box,
glides under door
and over threshold before
she performs the official rite,
will it seem worth it
as she accelerates into the night?

We may be sure,

for what judgement would be filed
against this contract
between a tooth fairy and her child?

THEIR MORBID MEASURINGS

Walking on my lonesome, Sunday morn,

beyond the average human's casual reach,

I chance upon a tree stump, newly felled,

two hundred circles wide, four seasons each.

Observing all those fractions of a life,

it sets my mind rotating over rings;

if someone chose to cleave my frame in two,

what units, in their morbid measurings,

would suit me well, convey essential thread,

give rationale for why I think this way?

Repentances from boundaries overstepped

or moments squandered, seeking, but afraid?

High hopes for all encountered could be true,

remotenesses would surely sooner teach

of why I'm walking lonesome, Sunday morn,

beyond the average human's casual reach.

STRANDED IN SEPIA

Alone now, in a fabricated time,
I wonder at the roles I've taken on.
Society is beautiful and blind,
its images abideable, but wrong.

My loved ones greet a boy who'll never be,
no need for confirmation of the view,
their negatives held under lock and key.
Sometimes I'm still convinced I know him too.

There calls a day for laughter and content,
when wild, unbroken dreams roll into town.
I whisper back, suspect I waste my breath.
Subdued upon each page, all answers drown.

Below the dust an envoy must descend;
inside a photo album I am found.

GALAXIES

There is a galaxy around us,
gleaming with the promise of activation.

We are beckoned by an array of subtle shades;
the loquacious linger of your stare,
the heaviness of the air as we pass close,
the quiver of my jawbone
as I tattle about the traffic on Market Way.

There is a galaxy we've always known
afraid to lose solidity,
extracting any victory it can;
a clarity in each goodbye
its influence is strong.

We are only pulled so viciously
because its core
suspects where we
belong.

THE WORD GOODBYE

We have zebras and antelopes, hedgehogs, deer,

we have rivers and streams flowing crystal clear,

we have drug-fuelled elation at eventide.

Who could ever believe in a world outside?

All brave explorations have slaved and failed,

stared into the void and the void prevailed.

No firelight flickers from distant hills,

no soul ever reached us and no soul will.

If you listen to reason, then chase it through,

you will sense which position endangers you.

Place your faith in the trusted, your gut knows why.

There are rumours of death in the word goodbye.

MY SOUNDTRACK TO A PICTURE FAR FROM CLEAR

There lives a song that many will have heard,
yet still this planet spins around the sun.
The record plays and by the middle third,
a chemical reaction has begun.

No longer do I lay upon my bed,
penned in by protocols and dull restraints,
but hover under greenwood canopy
no bulldozers or axes ever taint.

Arriving from a dozen different sides
come leprechauns and fairies, kings and queens.
A carnival procession for a bride
paraded through the centre of her scene.

An inner flame imbues a handsome face
with labyrinths the chosen might explore.
A vision of resolve bedecked in lace
with glovelette resting soft against her sword.

A minute takes an afternoon to pass

when each expectant face, excepting she,

looks to its left with lips that beg to ask

'What keeps the other newlywed to be?'

The fade arrives the moment that it must.

In sympathy, the actors crouch in fear.

I flip the vinyl, trying hard to trust

my soundtrack to a picture *far* from clear.

THE BORDERS OF MY MIND

I am nothing without the lure of a dwindling track
compressed by the sprawling of thistle, thorn and fern,
discovering secrets responsible persons lack
by limited compass and minimal self-concern.

Should someone be seeking escape from the life they've led
or someone get lost (as ostensibly I am now),
should others pay heed to their hearts, forsaking heads,
by vanishing ways are our destinies thrown in doubt.

When you pause to consider the likelihood of rain,
I will pass into places where nothing may fall nor shine.
You tether yourself to an innocent life mundane,
I wander untamed, possibilities thence combine,
persisting innocuous factors could explain
the menace still stayed near the borders of my mind.

BEATRICE IN THE DARK

The outside world came tugging on these sleeves,
his puppet-girl, my eyes-wide-open dreams.
'Go to the caves, go to the caves' she said;
no longer does she thrive beyond my head.

In love, in thrall to all things unexplained,
fresh eagerness arose and crashed as rain.
Returning stains of wisdom lost their hold,
with any fool's proposal I was sold.

Beware in walking sleep which route you stray
when every tooth that glitters judged for gold.

THE AXEMAN

Gather your loved ones

and press them well

to stem the trickling of their cares;

the axeman has not returned.

Tell all untameables

they venture out in packs

within the boundaries

of earshot and evelight.

Make a toast to his wife,

who must brave the scurries and screeches

alone tonight,

her gaze to a latchless door.

Collect our unsavoury tributes

and deliver them

over the brinks of abandoned paths;

commence the wait.

If silence endures

come autumn's prayer,

the rest of us will remember

that the axeman has not returned.

ALL UNTAMEABLES

You talk of danger, wield it like a club,
wax lyrical on places, trodden paths.
We come with different shoes and different feet;
we come with different urges, different hearts.

No honey-tongued address will make us hear,
no optical illusion make us see.
No bogeyman who preys on our mistakes
may sway what love intended us to be.

The murmur we should do as we are told
instruction we interpret liberally.

SCREW THE THORNS

Pick up those trembling, weary legs and run
while calories and limbs remain your own.
You've had one glimpse, you need to stop at one
else sanity decides to flee alone.
Go faster, tunnel vision, screw the thorns;
their gleeful scratches won't decide the day.
Duck under branch, make other gears once more
if just to make the noises go away.

Ten further yards, one last rebellious stride.
Come arid lungs, contrive to grant me breath.
I've almost reached my limits. Love, goodbye.
But what is this - no sound, have I been left?
Or does that thing still etched upon my eyes
find humour in a hopeful, playful death?

MOUSELIKE

I am a small, insignificant thing
forgetting what it was to be human,
focused on nothing grander
than staying alive.

I snuffle optimistically
through the undergrowth
for anything of sustenance
close to hand.

When I sense danger
I freeze,
flight-ready and stock-still,
itching to ascertain my fate.

ABOVE MY WATCHFUL GLARE

Come staggering on torpid limbs,
I wish to grasp another's name.
Ignore the furrows, crawl inside
the recess of my creaking frame.

These overtures are whisperings
I play to you from far below.
One ear against one mossy floor,
then drowsiness begins to show.

Your nemesis, my nobody,
will not be found, they would not dare
as now, involuntarily,
you sink above my watchful glare.

I ask no favour when you wake
and all I take, three locks of hair.

LAST WORDS

Whiskers, wanderings, cruelties, cares,
entrails, fingernails, locks of hair,
kidneys, clavicles, sweat glands, souls;
what has become of the things you stole?

Payments, barterings, entrées, sins
flung to the ends of distant limbs?
Trophies? Medicines? Calling Cards?
Focusing tools? Archaic arts?

Older than me, mayhaps as wise,
colder ones skulking deep inside.
How many miles does your sickness grow?
'Gainst wiser judgement, I wish to know.

MINIATURE GARDEN

I was born from an acorn, scattered far

by a seldom recounted shooting star.

Very near to this forest, I spied my way.

There are other ones like me, the ravens say.

I was never a boy, not exactly girl,

I will rarely be found in a concrete world.

These trees my pavilions, these lands my hosts,

I have witnessed your stewardships plenty close.

In the oldest of trunks, on the tallest fell,

where their eyes cannot see, but their hands may tell,

lies a miniature garden, intention's whir,

where the patterns take shape and the brushstrokes purr,

where the beasts of prostration long to fly,

where the flowers would swell to an unknown high

and the strands of my DNA still sing

for a faraway planet where queen was king.

HIS LAST RETURN

I'm waiting by the edge of wilderness,
the point from whence my love has disappeared.
If I must wait forever, then I must.

The woodland sneaks, replete with cleft and cave.
He pushed within, wee sacrificial lamb;
still soldiers on, unmindful of his cares.

Though I have often suffered, I am sure,
as I have seen the wildness in his heart,
these eyes will also witness love once more,

for I am clear of motive and of mind,
support him every twist and turn of his.
Somewhere beyond, he weighs my words for proof.

Our chimney smoke still rises high above.
I stoke the flames, peel carrots, warm the stove
and patiently await his last return.

BY PHONELIGHT

'Below' the aging, twisted 'oak',

I dare the monsters in,

invite my fingers

to dance by phonelight.

I come to this place

for contradictions,

mutations,

curveballs,

to offer memories

of my lost

for the aid of my must be found.

I ask that passers-by

mistake me for a glow-worm,

that I am left

to lever words like windows

until they open

onto the land I walk in dreams.

DUCK TO WATER

As I tiptoed in the dark,

I did not fear what I encountered,

only brooded on the shadows I revealed.

BENEATH THE DARKNESS

She treads the tree-lined evening way,
scattering spectres of the past
subordinated to her command.

The animals maintain their gaze
without fear,
accepting her
as one of their own.

She acknowledges kinship,
but wishes to be left
to her wounds,
believing there is work to be done
between them.

Ready for battle
should they refuse to be tamed,
a peaceful resolution remains her goal.

Beneath the darkness, there hides a gentle soul.

FIRELIGHT

I skirted round your sentries as you slept,
got lost in obfuscation and pretence,
laid stethoscope, with squinting for effect.
Beholden to the signal, recommenced,
slid deeper, using veins like waterslides,
past casual lacerations, tender grooves,
outran the spikes with furtive shadow strides
(though many faced within to tell the truth).

Beyond all else incongruous but me,
I found what I suspected all along;
soft pillows and a spot for sipping tea
by firelight both flickering and strong.

INTERSTELLAR

Autumn lands,

but the world beyond walls is calling.

I pry the skylight open,

then I shove my head above by way of answer.

Serenaded by the sounds of cars and lights of cranes,

I feel so very lonely

and alive.

I look up at the stars

and sense that one of them is yours,

almost prepared to believe the myth

that I could never reach it

as long as it's there

and you love me too.

RANDOM SHINY STAR

When you save up

your pathos

before you

wish upon

a random

shiny star,

does the star

get a say?

Or must it

shelve the succour

of all

less deserving cousins,

pool resources

under pity's

preening sway?

To the claim

'I'm a planet

with my own

motivations',

would you feel

inclined

to listen

anyway?

WRITE ANOTHER ENDING

I dream of turning feral

my later days,

of drinking

a little too much

and getting up to no good

with nobody watching;

even,

perhaps,

when they are.

Sometimes I come to question

who I'm procrastinating for.

Must I reach a certain age

to be dismissed

as harmless

and fly

below the radar,

now blessed

with inhibition fatigue

and no longer able to care

or will there come a time

when everyone

who made me feel ashamed

has blown elsewhere?

                                        Which gets me thinking

                                        'Why not start today?'

So I'm going to leave this poem

whilst I can,

but if you're worried

or unsettled

by the way

life seems to stand,

please don't hesitate

to write another ending.

ELF

Lost within a land of trees,
he came upon her gaze.
She no sooner seen than gone
and whether it was right or wrong,
he followed her away.

Examining where she had stood,
he spied a crimson hair.
Something which that face had kissed
was gathered soon within his fist;
he felt it twisting there.

Then in the distance, on the left,
he saw her arch a brow.
With languor that would vex a sloth,
she drifted through the undergrowth,
not his to wonder how.

He laboured with the wretched things
that some mistake for plants,
but when he reached the other side,
he found her arms were open wide
and starting to advance.

He bolted like the fawn he was
and never ventured back.
The crimson hair, you might have guessed,
submerged itself within his chest
and now has fallen slack.

AUGURY GREEN

I heard about a village green
that magic people know.
It rarely draws the urban type
and heather spreads along the track
they trod not long ago.

I wracked my brains and wrote my spells,
piled them to the roof
and when I thought I spied a glint,
I gathered up the best of them
and sought the green for proof.

It wasn't hard to find;
I met some folk along the way.
They offered me some pixie dust,
pointed out the quickest route
and led me well astray.

The village green was full of fools.
I studied them with glee -
illusionists and sorcerers,
contortionists and acrobats,
the conjuress and me.

I made the green my second home
a year along the line
and though the heather spotted path
mislaid the best of city hearts,
it found and conquered mine.

SWIRLING IN SYNC

Sometimes it's okay to be alone

when the stars

and the clouds

and the moon

intermingle in just the right way,

when the warm summer air

is laced with familiar scents

from an unfamiliar clime

and the hoots

and the howls

and the cries

are everywhere,

but not there

and you talk of the past

with the trees

and the stems

and the leaves

all swirling in sync with their peers,

whispering

'You can forget them

now you have us.

Nothing else matters but here.'

FOUR FISTS UNCURL

We surface, bruised and battered, but alive.
Protectively, you scout the world outside,
contrive to sound convincing when you say
'Perhaps, for now, The Demon's gone away.'

Attempting to accept, confused and scared,
I clamber from this refuge, mutely stare.
Slow seeping through, the passing of the squall,
we squeeze together, let the teardrops fall.

A boldness in the woods appears to grow
when crocus lifts its nose above the snow;
an underbrush alive with smaller feet
that long to run, for now remain discreet.

As if to catch my soul, your eyes are cast,
entreating me 'This has to be the last.'
I feel the words inside me calcify.
Four fists uncurl, you lead us back to life.

BECAUSE WE MUST

On days when grasping just a glimpse
retreating from periphery,
you turned around to open air;
not every time was make-believe.
We have a home I think you'd like,
a softening which might be earned.
Our feral kin may wander through,
but as it stands, you cannot learn.

All wilderness retrained and sold,
unwilling subjects ground to dust.
You have your ways as we have ours,
we disappear because we must,
yet seek no thunder from the gods
and take no vengeance as we might.
We live the way we've always lived,
untouchable, beyond your sight.

A DRAGON I MUST SLAY

These neverending quests our human way,
ungrateful to the fly upon the wall.
I love you so much more than I can say.

While pleasantly the most of me delays,
your little spoon (so sound asleep we fall),
serene has never been the mortal's way.

In slumber, many souls remain awake.
Immune to all repose, impatience crawls,
insists there dwells a dragon I must slay

and I, by nature, softly led astray,
already there, soon spoiling for a brawl,
dive in when more important things decay.

You stretch your drowsy arm across my waist
and swiftly, there is nothing else at all.
There must have been a point to being brave.

I stir, wild visions chomping on my brain,
press onwards for the cold adjoining hall.
This stubborn voice will never go away,
forgets I love you more than I can say.

REBELLIONS

He struggles with pyjamas, brushes teeth,
succumbs to bed, considers counting sheep,
looks over to the bookshelf, night must wait.
In sleepy heads lie other realms awake.

She smiles towards the shoppers wanting help;
when duty done, returns to stacking shelves
where managers will struggle to detain
meandering well stocked and fully trained.

I keep it light at dinner, then the news,
the tanks, the bombs, explosions, turning screws.
Dejection stoked and situation scanned
(my study desk awaits, escape long planned),
find happiness exploring other realms,
considering a different quiet stand.

WITHOUT YOUR FIRM ASSENT

It's strange, when you have dreamt of this for days,
some sentimental duty still delays
the very things we should be grasping for.
I offer revelation, never war.

You hide behind abstractions and conceits;
where dirt prevails, proclaim unsullied sheets.
Draw closer to devotion's kryptonite.
Without your firm assent, I will not bite.

The time has come to pick forbidden fruits
or suffer what you tell yourself is right.

PALE MOONLIGHT

Confusticated, begging to believe
contentedness, my life should interweave.
Deliverance already underway,
pale moonlight through the clouds, companions fay.

When briar straddled path, I shambled on,
unsure from whom resolve was siphoned from,
unkeeled by inclination's to and fro,
disciple under dust-reflected glow.

You linger on the stage for long enough,
it tempts someone above to steal the show.

THE SCENT OF HIS JUMPER

I'm not afraid

of these blades

nor the teeth

they shelter

and if I

should perish,

I will not flinch,

but wolf

whatsoever remains,

for as long

as the scent

of his jumper

lingers on,

I'll find radiance

probing the corners

of the most

uninviting place.

FAIRIES EXIST

Some people dream of sunset red skies,
never quite reach them, never know why,
happy to sing society's mores.
Fairies exist and I will be yours.

Other folks' loves are lost in retreat,
scattered and scarred by first springtime heat,
yearn for the forest, hide from the trees.
Fairies exist and so does the breeze.

Foolish lips falter, slowly turn old,
grow to abide, then worship the cold,
comfortably coy without getting kissed.
When will they learn that fairies exist?

Bitter mouths prowl the touchlines and laugh,
always the editors, rarely the drafts.
Leave them to prowl, no need for applause.
Fairies exist and I will be yours.

SOME PRETTY FLOWERS

Ten thousand shades of August climbing high,
so many nerves, two beating reasons why.
Lush crimson purples beckon us within,
some pretty flowers veil delightful things.

At last, we join, appending hues of rose,
task lilies by the edge to guard these clothes
and now, beneath a quilted, crawling roof,
the bugs alone bear witness to our truth.

SMALLER SHIFTS OF FATE

The blue car in the drive is back,
no plans for driving out,
a life unlost until it's gone
whatever people shout.

To think that we were standing here
slim happenstance before,
same DNA, same skin and bones,
same dreams of nothing more,

crude cardboard figures paralysed
by unimportant things
like dignity, propriety,
the paucity of wings,

when now, without an answer due
on how, exactly why,
the atoms have been rearranged -
crude cardboard granted life -

aligning to each other's cells,
transformed by ebb and flow,
forgetting what we sensed in freeze
slim happenstance ago,

then pausing for a little prayer
to smaller shifts of fate,
all fingers crossed they get to you
before it gets too late.

BOY NUMBER ONE

A funny sort of friendship
started maiden day in Mayfield.
Seems lazy, but I won't distil
exactly why I liked you.
We don't all want to know how magic is done.

I went to yours from time to time.
We kept ourselves amused with games
but couldn't find an awful lot to say.

Once,
when we were about to part,
we stood on the upstairs landing
and the fleeting thought of kissing you
came in, said sorry and left.

Another parting, in school,
absentmindedly called 'I love you'.
The two of us kept walking
and are walking to this day.

A STILLNESS YOU MUST HAVE TOUCHED

The village unworthy,

their gaze unceasing,

all boatlets run aground, beyond repair,

you left us to ourselves

and joined the wild,

hoping to find in silence

what was lost in a crowded room.

Part of me feels envy

for a stillness you must have touched

upon its passing.

We almost pressed it together once,

somewhere between

the barley field

and the baffling winter sky.

Now this world you choose to flee from

pulls you closer

as you evade

all risk of love.

HERE I LINGER DREAMING

The woodpeckers are pecking at their trees,
the bumblebees chase nectar where they will,
the squirrels vex their predators with glee
and here I linger dreaming on this hill.
The upland writhes, alive with industry,
the schemer seeking ends to be fulfilled.

One lazy, yellow Bunsen sheds its rays
on flimsy limbs outsplayed against the grass.
Two cloudlets overthin for making shade
fail gamely to reanimate the past.
Three atlas moths emerge, then entertain,
fly high and for an afternoon would last.

MORNINGTIME

On staggering towards the midnight bells,
that simple, convoluted shade of man
may dwindle, then dissolve within his mind.

Too busy for display, more bitter still,
a prisoner to everything that was,
the flickers from the present fade unseen.

Forgetting to unclench one cramping fist,
he wanders back to cloudy, sunny days
of kites aloft and Rubicons uncrossed.

His morningtime, before the lights went out,
where never came a pause for second thought,
he might have been a person they could love.

A SAILOR'S HANDBOOK

Sometimes to sweat for land is not enough,
the gloomy thoughts prevail (they like it rough).
Sometimes I pick a fight with me by stealth,
tonight you shall be gentle with yourself.

The best of us despair so far from shore,
observing melancholy's overtures.
Catharsis that much harder to distil,
but moping only makes salt water spill.

Beyond bewildered fogs of seasons through,
the lighthouse of the present covets you.
Adrift amidst the past, a boat might sink -
write tragedies in pencil, not with ink.

When waves of trepidation crash your bow,
just bide your time, keep steering anyhow.
Upon firm subjugation of the sea,
head over to the bar and ask for me.

STREWN

Humans build their navies,
plotting from the sands.
Waves were made for crashing,
sink a thousand plans.

Childhood dreams aborted
with the ocean swell,
strewn amongst the seaweed,
only time will tell.

Hiding in the branches,
questing different ways,
motivation lingers,
hunger ever stays.

Jealousy a mouthful,
stronger men have choked.
Hopelessness eludes me,
scourge of grounded folk.

Stare towards Polaris
through the breaks in leaves,
steadying my sailors,
rising from my knees.

Soon the year for wresting
from the current's rage,
dictionary open,
pencil on the page.

BEGIN TO KNOW

Steal out and take a chance,
past the wardens of this keep.
There is nothing to be won
repretending what has flown.

The hearth forever lit,
fingers long to interlace
far beyond the shallow scopes
of all introspective fears

and if you can't do it for yourself,
then do it just for them.

Breathing deep December air,
then reoffering as mist,
you will glance up ahead,
begin to know.

NOW

Freed from the hurricanes
of past failures
blasting me backwards then,
my leaves coalesce in the present,
wishing no longer to be distracted
by lovelorn prose.

Gliding across the threshold
minus a caution,
missing all care,
believing which fate awaits me there
is unsealed,
I can but smile,

because when the future comes,
it will be altered,
because on this day,
I delivered myself
to now.

SOLITAIRE

On wresting your attention back
to moments I would love to share,
reluctantly I recognise
tonight I'm playing solitaire.

It's like the pixies come for you,
removing all but husk by stealth.
Officially, you're sitting down,
yet always spinning someplace else.

What kind of rupture would it take
to punctuate absorption's bonds,
return you now to Planet Earth?
And where might you be coming from?

You drift through time as well as space,
by grand design, please say I'm wrong?

A JOURNEY I MIGHT CALL HOME

Unarmed, unfollowed, unscared, alone,

stretching a journey I might call home,

pause where the oaks cast reds and browns,

look to the sunset, lay me down,

narrow my eyes so I just see shapes,

close them for real, let the darkness take,

laugh at the wind's most charming lies,

sleep till the daylight next arrives.

Lift from the petals around my knees,

thousands of flowers where once were trees,

finches assemble a rainbow crew,

emperors flutter, then fade from view.

Circling thermals, the corvids climb,

collectively nouning their favourite crimes.

Blossoming peacocks set their stalls.

Far in the distance, my dovelet calls.

Unarmed, unfollowed, unscared, alone,

resuming a journey I might call home.

THIS DISCONNECTED COMPANY

Perhaps there is no answer
as to why we feel this way,
fantabulous and threadbare,
so corrosive, yet so calm.

Relentless with passivity,
though tremulous in passion.
Apostles to our poetry,
distrusting of our goals.

Was ever any one of us
from former times of valour
united on a battlefront,
unguarded at their core?

We wield a kind of bravery
advancing with our questions,
this disconnected company,
together through the smoke.

SEBASTIAN, STEVEN

Sebastian plays with his age-old cards,
shuffles again when defeat stings hard,
spurns all suggestions for blaming tools,
tries not to worry who frames the rules,
plagued by the doubt that weighs him down,
stalling escape near the edge of town,
'What if convictions are only bluffs?
Search in their eyes and I can't find love?'

Held by a vision, he makes his stand,
carrying fears through a distant land.

Steven unfurls at the sounds decline -
silence condones what he casts behind -
sticks to the script when the darkness chafes,
pictures his absence, then knows them safe,
never to finish the game begun,
never restarting, perhaps with one,
burning propellants, however slight,
nursing a dream in refracted light.

Held by a vision, he makes his stand,
carrying fears through a distant land.

Seven years later and six years wed,
Sebastian and Steven awake in bed,
folded together in love so sure,
feeling impossible, tasting more.
Nothing impossibly far from reach,
thousands of bottles still fringe the beach,
millions of stars in a prayer-filled sky
twinkling on leaf and bough,
you
and I.

Held by a vision, we make our stand,
carrying fears through a distant land.

ABANDONED SHACK

I see a box still ribboned
in a world without surprise,
two distant restaurant eyes,
my fairy tale's absent page.

I see a hand I would lunge for
should the branches beneath me crack,
self-secluded abandoned shack
unbarred to a storm-drenched soul.

I see a route stumbled onto
in a future I thought had none,
this cosseted curse undone,
a view beyond pastel shades.

THE SUPPLENESS OF CURFEWS

I love the gentle gleam
that comes through friendship found
as though each discovers
a different door
to a room that has always beckoned.

In your old, decrepit car
that would soon be ours,
we scrutinised
the suppleness of curfews,
talking
of all the lies we saw
and a promise
we'd fight them together.

The gentle gleam
resurfaced
just for us,
announcing no arrivals,
only beginnings.

DAWN

There is an edge

to our infant sky

never seen before,

as though you

stole away

life's pessimistic lens

whilst I was drowning

in daymares;

nestled yourself

in their stead.

Now I bask
within the beams
of passers-by,
watch indifferently
as rooftop gargoyles
flutter with their dread,
silence myself
so as not to scare
a cautious pair of eyes,
knowing I
will proffer them
this gently extended hand,
any place
in my sky
their fantasies
can tread.

NOW THAT WE ARE BIRDIES TOO

I find you there amongst the foliage,
relaxed, as if you guessed I'd be along.
The rustle of your flitter round my perch
proves every fear I've ever had was wrong.

Those funny little birdy squawks and squeaks,
so ominously shrill before today,
make music now that we are birdies too.
We stretch our fledgling wings, then fly away.
No limits to the worlds before our eyes
and only nature's laws we shall obey.

LABYRINTHIAN

Risking our necks for the slightest chances,
running a mile from all fleeting glances,
no one can tell me love weaves its docile course.

Drafting crude letters at crazy hours,
swallowing potions, scaling towers,
restless, reluctant and always, forever, yours.

Dressed to the nines, pretentions naked,
fears crying out, hopes understated,
playing with chips I cannot afford to lose.

Sifting through safes, then under floorboards,
pondering facts, maintaining scoreboards,
making it up and looking to you for clues.

Clueless as me, you shrug your shoulders.

Left on its own, intention moulders,

innocent slave to wandering plot's design.

Let us be bold, obscure inventions,

free of all taste, soft grey conventions.

Anything under your duvet would prove divine.

THANK YOU

Thank you
for the heady days
of half-knowings,
for the you's and me's
of uncertainties
that hover
around our hearts.

Thank you
for the starts
that may never finish,
all wisdoms diminished
by wayward butterfly wings,
for the singing of songs
too shy
for a true love's dotings.

Thank you

for the hopeless hopings

that come with these conditions,

rude mutterings,

split decisions,

the staggers and sways

of fate and fortune's

tease.

Thank you

for these idiocies,

strange explorations,

secondments above our stations.

Thank you

for their realisations

we trust will arrive

on cue.

I MET A WITCH

When I was young, I jumped from grace
and secret things clicked into place.
Like apple falling from the tree,
I met a witch who poisoned me.

He'd practised long his casual airs,
haphazard hopes, indifferent stares.
I guessed them for a slim disguise
to shield the darkness from these eyes,

but darkness came and came in barbs,
such vitriol they made me laugh.
Offense was feigned, though soon was gone,
betrayed a smile that ranted on.

Emboldened now, from poison blurred,
I watched as something warmer stirred,
assumed control, so little fuss,
till we were drunk, the both of us.

Sung catchy songs still no one knows,
then skipped around on twinkletoes.
For shallow space, we shone too bright,
cavorted out and faced the night.

The folks who saw all shook their heads,
consumed by existential dread.
In every spear ill temper threw
lay fear of sipping poison too.

Unopened minds, our hearts laid bare,
yet having too much fun to care;
on broomstick steed, away from land,
more keenly drawn by magic's hand,

when I was young, I jumped from grace
and secret things clicked into place.
Like apple falling from the tree,
I met a witch who poisoned me
with love.

DARK, ANCIENT WOODS

In middle school huddles, the other boys talked
about the rituals enacted in dark, ancient woods -
perhaps that's where they disappeared.

The door knocked.

I rose, stretched my back and went outside.
You whispered you had come,
then took me near and far away,
from road to trodden path to hidden hollow.

I went along
because it was time
and you were you.

I stood there, braced for harshness, death and ridicule.
None came,
just a gentle, faltering hand
flicking a rusty, cobwebbed switch from off to on.

I don't remember letting go,
but I remember your soft cries
as you told of how you'd circled before
without daring to venture in.

I kissed you and said 'We're here.'

I KNEW

I had a dream (a real one for a change),

I'd wandered off and paced the London streets

with many things uncertain on my mind,

distrust for every citizen complete.

Though wantonly dispirited and lost,

the solace of the railway station came.

Inside, a payphone, rummaged without coins,

asked 'Please reverse the charges?' Gave your name.

You answered, all confusion in your tone,

like every fundamental ran askew

and only one event would put them right;

on hearing it was me, all fear subdued,

talked nonsense that could only have been joy.

Immersed in my unconsciousness, I knew.

PRIVILEGE

There's beauty in the sparkle of those eyes,

a privilege I'd never disavow.

Some wager the return upon your stake

is not enough, but love me anyhow.

ISLAND

Laying low was fine for a while,

then shyness chose to sail away,

having long outlasted the finer points of reason.

I found myself adrift

above a lake of possibility,

squinting upwards toward the brightness of the sun.

Acknowledging the flimsiness

that preys upon these vehicles,

saw clearer than my plans to last forever.

At peace and still adventuresome,

I steered against the undertow,

remembering our oft-imagined island.

ONE TINY ANONYMOUS SPECK

On the main road,

twice a day,

we'd pass our venerable tree

standing alone in the poppy field

and every time,

our eyes would stray

with wonder

towards its towering grandeur,

verticality of stance,

without any sense of envy,

seeing nothing to be gained

from the upright life

that leads us to a solitary death.

I am a gnarly twisted shrub

and your limbs were never destined for straightness,

so if you find me leaning your way

until we are nearly touching,

there is no malfunction,

I'm just hoping

one day

we can fade and fall apart together,

one tiny anonymous speck

blending into the background of our choice.

FINIS

I'm tracing back the breadcrumb trail
once scattered from this fevered mind.
However many dreams I stray,
my fate with yours lies intertwined.
Some loves can never bend, they break,
some lovers hold a different kind.

I see you now in beige and black,
the keeper of my let's pretends.
Above, astride, below your lap
are several more deserving friends.
Still, every fantasist must have
one place their favourite story ends.

ACKNOWLEDGEMENTS

Thank you to Jane for everything you bring to aspiring writers like me – your true illustrative excellence and your eye for artwork that will enhance our vision; your enthusiasm (when you're sending me all those opportunities you've come across, it's like I have an agent and I love it!) and also your good-natured warmth that makes you such a joy to work with.

Thank you to all the writers on Twitter and Instagram who have encouraged and inspired me. I'm perhaps more of a 'hide yourself away from the world' person by nature and to have a sense of community and belonging has really brought me out of my shell.

I would especially like to thank Susan Richardson, who was cheering me on from my first published poem and who I am very lucky to have as a friend.

Finally, my husband Matt who moves heaven and earth to keep a household running smoothly while I'm worrying about whether to use a comma or a semicolon. I love you.

Lawrence x

List of Previously Published Poems

Our Discordant Song: The Dawntreader 63

You Needn't Search Alone: DarkWinter

My Soundtrack to a Picture Far From Clear, One Tiny Anonymous Speck: Fevers of the Mind

Mouselike: Toil and Trouble (Issue 02, Animals)

His Last Return, Beneath the Darkness: Roi Fainéant Press

Interstellar: Soft Star (Issue Two, Aurora)

Swirling in Sync, Dark Ancient Woods: Dreich (Number 5, Season 6; Number 9, Season 4)

Fairies Exist, Some Pretty Flowers: Poetry as Promised (Valentines Day Issue 2023)

Boy Number One: The Rainbow Poems (2022, Issue 1)

The Stillness You Must Have Touched: The Madrigal (Volume vi, Epiphany)

ABOUT LAWRENCE MOORE

Lawrence Moore has lived in the coastal city of Portsmouth, England since birth and shares a house overlooking Kingston Cemetery with his husband Matthew and their nine mostly well behaved cats.

A firm believer in environmentalism and animal welfare, he spent many teenage days involved in protesting and direct action.

He has felt an affinity for poetry from a young age and wrote periodically down the years before committing to it in his early forties.

His poems have appeared in publications including Sarasvati, Fahmidan Journal, Pink Plastic House, Green Ink Poetry, Dreich and The Madrigal.

He released a debut chapbook, *Aerial Sweetshop*, with Alien Buddha Press in January 2022.

You can find him on Twitter under the handle @LawrenceMooreUK.

About Jane Cornwell

Jane is an artist, illustrator and book designer. After responding to Paul Brookes call out for an artist to provide 30 prompt artworks for a National Poetry Month Ekphrastic Challenge, 2020, she discovered that she really enjoys reading and listening to poetry. She realised she could give some deserving poets the chance to get their work published and set up her own small poetry press, Jane's Studio Press. Since, she's collaborated with Paul Brookes, Samantha Terrell and Susan Richardson to create poetry books. Committing to producing these books in her free time means Jane has to keep her drawing and painting skills up, and she enjoys working in a collaborative way with her chosen poets.

Jane has exhibited with the RSW at the National Gallery of Scotland, The Big Art Show, Glasgow, SSA, Knock Castle Gallery, Aberdeen Artists Society, The Glasgow Group, Paisley Art Institute, MacMillan Exhibition at Bonhams, Edinburgh, The House For An Art Lover, Pittenweem Arts Festival, Compass Gallery, The Revive Show, East Linton Art Exhibition and Strathkelvin Annual Art Exhibition.

Jane is a member of Publishing Scotland and the Association of Illustrators. She graduated with a BA(Hons) in Design from the Glasgow School of Art, age 20.

Her website is: www.janecornwell.co.uk.

Printed in Great Britain
by Amazon